# 2 GRRRLS

## What A Friend!

## Friendship Tips from 2 GRRRLS™

by Kristen Kemp

**SCHOLASTIC INC.**

New York   Toronto   London   Auckland   Sydney
Mexico City   New Delhi   Hong Kong

No part of this publication may be reproduced in whole or in part, or stored in a retrieval system or transmitted in any form, or by any means, electronic, mechanical, photocopying, recording, or otherwise, without written permission of the publisher. For information regarding permission, write to Scholastic Inc., Attention: Permissions Department, 555 Broadway, New York, NY 10012.

ISBN 0-439-20893-9

Cover and interior design by Louise Bova.

Copyright © 2000 by 2 GRRRLS, Inc.

Published by Scholastic Inc. All rights reserved.

SCHOLASTIC and associated logos are trademarks and/or registered trademarks of Scholastic Inc. 2 GRRRLS and all related characters, logos and elements are trademarks and/or registered trademarks of 2 GRRRLS, Inc. BE THE GIRL YOU WANNA BE is a trademark of 2 GRRRLS, Inc.

12 11 10 9 8 7 6 5 4 3 2 1          0 1 2 3 4 5/0

Printed in the U.S.A.          40
First Scholastic printing, September 2000

# Table of Contents

**Hi, Hello, How Are Ya?** . . . . . . . . .5

## Chapter 1
What Kind of Friend Are You? . . . . . .10

## Chapter 2
Picking Your Pals . . . . . . . . . . . . . .18

## Chapter 3
The Best Stuff About Friends! . . . . . . .29

## Chapter 4
Absolutely Fabulous Ways
to Be a Better Buddy . . . . . . . . . . . .33

## Chapter 5
Friendship Fixes . . . . . . . . . . . . . . .37

## Chapter 6
You Must Have a Lot of Friends!
Here's How to Hang With 'Em! . . . . . .46

## Chapter 7
Real Answers for Real Pal Problems . .54

**See Ya! Bye!** . . . . . . . . . . . . . . . .64

# Hi, Hello, How Are Ya?

A girl needs friends. Friends make you feel warm and fuzzy. They're great for hanging out with and for sharing secrets. And friends are always there to lift slumping spirits and to make you laugh. Everyone needs tons of friends, friends, friends!

But having great girlfriends means you gotta *be* a great girlfriend. Sometimes it just comes naturally. Other times being a fab friend is easier said than done. But don't worry. You can learn how to be a best bud and find out what it means to be a real Grrrls' Girl.

This book will give you tons of friendship tips — from making friends, to helping them out of a problem, to having tons of fun. So go ahead. Get your girlfriends and get reading! Find out what friends are for!

## Grrrls' Girl (gurlz' gurl):

(n) a young woman who is a friend no matter what; who is always loyal and respectful; who does things for or with her friends; who is her own awesome self; who is always superkind; who is someone other girls like to like; who is smart and loves to learn; who is self-assured and independent.

## Meet the Grrrls' Girls from 2 Grrrls:

## Rella: Girlie Girl

People call me a princess because I'm a real girlie girl. I just love being a girl — it's so much fun! I'm always supersweet to my friends and I'm real careful not to say anything that will hurt their feelings. I like taking care of all my friends. I just can't stand it when my friends are unhappy, so I always go out of my way to cheer them up! (And I admit it: I also have a soft spot for mushy movies and fluffy puppies.)

# Tutti: Glamour Girl

I love my friends because they're so beautiful – inside and out! I'm not afraid to show my friends how I feel. Usually I'm very happy and talkative, but when I'm sad, watch out 'cause here come the tears! What else? Oh, yeah. People might accuse me of being bossy, but I'm not – honest! It's just that, well, I like to come up with all sorts of fun things for my friends and me to do.

# Roxy: Groovy Girl

I'm a great bud! I love giving my friends advice, and I love to make them smile — and laugh a lot, too. (My friends say I'm the best when they need a pep talk!) I believe that I can do anything I want to do, and so can my friends. I always make my friends feel extra good by telling them, "You go, girl!"

# Looie: Go-for-It! Girl

I might be a little quiet when people first meet me, but when they get to know me, they find out that I'm a true friend. I don't have a ton of friends — I'm always busy playing soccer, working on my computer, and reading books — but I'm really loyal to the ones I do have. And I'd never let anyone mess with a friend of mine — no way! I'm always there to stick up for my friends!

# Chapter 1

# What Kind of Friend Are You?

What kind of bud are you? Answer the sets of questions on the next few pages and find out!

* Has anyone ever told you that you do more for your friends than you do for yourself?
* Have you been known to cry when you get supersweet cards from your buds?
* Do you tend to take care of all your friends?
* Would you rather eat mud than say something nasty about someone, even if they deserve it?
* Do you hardly ever, ever meet someone you don't like?

If this sounds like you, then you're a sweet and sensitive friend. Your friends look to you for advice and comfort. They know they can count on you for anything! They probably consider you the glue that holds your pals together.

Rella is this kind of friend.

# Meet Rella

I'm sweet – at least I think I am! I love doing things for my friends. They know they can call me anytime for anything –even if it's midnight or six in the morning. I am there for them forever! I'm the kind of girl who likes to meet people. I am nice to everyone – I don't think I even know how to be mean.

I spend a lot of time looking through magazines, then drawing the clothes that I see. I hope to be a famous fashion designer one day, so I have already started practicing. I even learned to sew – and am getting much better at it lately!

What else can I say about me? My mom says I'm very neat and kind of particular. I don't know about the last part, but I always make my bed and straighten my room. No one even has to tell me to!

## Fave Friendship Quote:

*"We'll always be together!"*

**Check out these questions.**

**If you answer yes and think they describe you, read on to find out more about your friendship style.**

✻ Are you the leader of your pack of pals?

✻ Do you think that some people might not understand you?

✻ Have you ever been accused of being bossy?

✻ Are you the supercreative one of your bunch who always thinks up wild new things to do?

✻ Do you love your friends because they're so beautiful on the inside?

If this sounds like you, then you're a kind-hearted and good all-around friend. You are very popular and tons of fun, too! No one can come up with crazy stuff like you do!

Tutti is this kind of friend.

# Meet Tutti

People call me gorgeous because I believe that beauty comes from within! I try to live by that rule.

I am a drama queen! I even want to be an actress one day. I love actresses who play strong girls and who know what they want. I like to think me and my friends are like that.

Even though I'm very outgoing, sometimes I worry too much about whether people understand me. I guess I'm just self-conscious that way. I may seem totally confident and happy on the outside, but I'm sometimes feeling very different on the inside. I just try not to show it.

I am sincere and nice. Sure, I can be a little bit bossy. But I don't mean to be! Also, I would never do anything to hurt my friends' feelings. I think that's because I get my feelings hurt so easily. I am so sensitive. But I'm also creative and colorful. I like to think up new things and try them all the time.

## Fave Friendship Quote:

*"You're nothing without your friends!"*

**Check out these questions.**

**If you answer yes and think they describe you, read on to find out more about your friendship style.**

* Are you the one your pals turn to when they're blue?

* Do you always remind your pals how wonderful they are and never miss a chance to cheer them on?

* Do people describe you as positive and energetic?

* Do you like to try new things almost all the time?

* Are you a total talker? Do you tell tons of jokes?

If this sounds like you, then you have a wonderful gift — you make people smile. They bust their guts when you're around. And they also look to you for serious talks when they are down. And you're so thoughtful — you go out of your way to make sure your pals are always in a good mood and feeling great about themselves.

Roxy is this kind of friend.

# Meet Roxy

I can't help it – I like to laugh. And I'm a bit of a talker, too. I can go on and on and on about anything. I don't think I am quiet or shy at all. So I guess it makes sense that I would love to be a VJ one day. I am way into singing and all kinds of music, too. Sometimes I write my own tunes and send them to my favorite divas. One day I hope those super singers use one! I just know they will – I just know it! I go to their Web sites every day to check out what they're doing. I told you I'm a dreamer, right?

I really love clothes. My grandma Nellie used to work at a big fashion magazine in New York City – she's even taken me there to see it. So we like to shop for the most stylish clothes. We love to be up-to-date and superhip. We're both very stubborn, though. That's something I'm trying to work on. I always like to be as happy and positive as humanly possible!

I love to find new stuff to do. Also, I live to cheer my friends on! I believe you can be whatever you want to be. I always say, "You go, girl!" to my closest friends. When my friends are down, they can count on me to help them get back up. I try to be sensitive – and not to joke when stuff's not funny. So I listen really hard.

**Fave Friendship Quote:**
*"You get by with a little help from your friends!"*

**Check out these questions.**

**If you answer yes and think they describe you, read on to find out more about your friendship style.**

* Does it take a long time to get to know you?
* Are you a little quiet and reserved when you first meet someone new?
* Do you speak up to anyone when something's going on that isn't right?
* If someone tells you a secret, do you never, ever tell another soul?
* Has anyone ever told you that you're incredibly loyal?

If this sounds like you, then you might be a tough one to get to know. That's just because you're a little on the quiet side. But just because you're shy doesn't mean you're not a great friend! To you, BFF means Best Friends Forever, and you mean it. You'll stand by your friends until the end!

Looie is this kind of friend.

# Meet Looie

I am not much of a talker – so I'm really glad I get to write this stuff down. Anyway, I'm not scared of anything. It could be because I have three big brothers. I like to play sports – especially soccer – and I think spiders are cool. I even take my pet iguana on walks sometimes. When I'm not practicing soccer, I'm usually hangin' on my computer. I just taught myself how to make websites. I love doing that! I also like to read and study. I know it sounds crazy, but I love doing homework and taking tests. I am always helping my friends with their school stuff.

Like my friends, I am a real Grrrls' Girl. I don't have tons of buds, but I'm very true to the ones I have. I am very honest – and sometimes too blunt. But I like to think I am the most loyal and dedicated friend that anyone could ever have. (I hope I am!) And I am the best when it comes to keeping secrets. I stick up for my friends no matter what – that's the only time I really speak up.

**Fave Friendship Quote:**
*"Friends are forever!"*

# Chapter 2

# Picking Your Pals

Meeting new people and making the effort to learn things about them is what helps friendships grow and grow! But feeling comfy with someone you don't know doesn't happen overnight. You have to take your time and get to know each and every individual. Remember: Every person is a hidden gem. You just have to take time to find her sparkly parts!

Also, you need to know that you don't have to be friends with a person who's exactly like you. And you don't have to only hang out with the same kind of girl all the time. It's great to be friends with all different types of people. Each girl has something unique to bring to the friendship. Maybe one girl is a dreamer while another is more of a realist. But both can benefit from hanging out with each other — differences actually make friendships much more special.

# We're Perfect!

Sometimes friendship just happens! That's how it was for us. It started before I was born! My mom and Tutti's mom are the best of buddies. They went to grade school and high school and college together! They were at each other's weddings, and then they even had their kids around the same time. That ended up being Tutti and me, by the way! When we were babies, people thought that we were twins. Tutti and I shared the same playpens and toys and crayons. We became the best of friends, just like our moms. Lucky, huh?

We met Roxy when we were in the first grade. We all took dance classes together. I remember Tutti dancing like Janet Jackson even then. She was so good at the shuffle-hop-step that the teacher asked her to do her own solo act. She is just a natural-born star! Meanwhile,

I was too into our ballet tutus and costumes to care about the actual dancing! Anyway, Roxy was in our class, and she started hanging out with Tutti a lot. They were both dancing divas. I was so jealous at first. But once I talked to Roxy, I couldn't help but love her, too! She always made me laugh, and she was supercaring. So the three of us started doing everything together.

Then, in the second grade, there was a new girl in my class. Her name was Looie, and she was shy. I thought she looked like she needed a friend. So I invited her to my house one day along with Roxy and Tutti. Looie was so different from us! She knew about games we'd never played, and she let us borrow her favorite books. We loved her immediately. And I guess she loved us, too! We're still the best of buds!

# Friendship Tip! Just So Ya Know!

That's how friendships are — sometimes they just click. Even when everyone is very different, each person has a lot to share! Rella is always taking the time to do stuff for others. Tutti is the creative drama girl who comes up with lots of fun and silly ideas. Roxy makes people smile, and she helps her friends feel better when they are down. Looie has a lot of guts — she sticks up for everyone — and she makes her friends try new things. And just like lots of groups of friends, they have one another in common. They appreciate others for who they are and how they're different.

Rella, Tutti, Roxy, and Looie have learned one great thing: Having friends is an investment. When you give, you always get back something really great!

# How You Can Make New Buddies, Too!

The Grrrls' Girls teamed up to write you this list. Here are a few things they've done to make a new pal or two:

## 1. Take a class!

I love to act, so I signed up for drama classes at our little town's theater. It's fun! I've met lots of new people who are as passionate about acting as I am. Even though my Grrrls are great, they're not into acting the way I am. But my theater friends are!

— *Tutti*

## 2. Sign up for more clubs at school.

I say hi to lots of people because I know them from swimming club and the student council. If I have time, I like to sign up for anything and everything! It's not only a great way to meet new people, but it's also a fabulous way to learn about something and be part of a team.

— *Roxy*

### 3. Carry your favorite mag — or say hello to someone who's carrying a mag that interests you!

Carry a copy of *Teen People* or *Twist* and have it in your hand when you're walking in the hall between classes or in the cafeteria. It's a great way to start chatting because people will be curious about what you're reading. On the flip side, you could always make the first move and say hi to someone who's carrying a mag that you think is cool. First, walk up to her at lunch and say hello. You'd be surprised how nice people are — and how they really would like to talk with you. Then, if you run out of things to talk about, mention something you've read about a fave celeb, for example. When I do this, next thing I know, I've met someone new!

— *Rella*

### 4. Go to summer camp — alone!

I was not very excited about it, but my dad made me go to camp by myself. He sent me to soccer camp last summer for one full week. He says he went when he was a kid — so he wanted me to have the same experience. Well, I ended up having a blast! Now I have lots of pen pals who I get to see every summer. (And

my dad told me he met one of his best buds at sleep-away camp, and they still keep in touch!)

— *Looie*

## 5. Join the local library's book club.

Okay, I have to give Looie credit for this one. She signed us up for the library book club. We read a book a month and then go to the library to talk about it. It's so cool! And I meet a lot of really smart and interesting kids. We always go for milkshakes at the end! My mom and I are even thinking about joining a book club together. She's my friend, too!

— *Tutti*

## 6. Volunteer!

I met my friend Matt at a charity car wash. I volunteered – and you know I don't like to get my clothes one bit dirty, but it was a blast. Plus, we helped make a lot of money for charity. While soaping up the cars, I started talking to Matt. Needless to say, I have a new crush!

— *Rella*

## 7. Hang out in a new neighborhood.

My aunt Shady lives about thirty minutes away, and I used to go there on the weekends a lot. I would ride my bike and go to the park. Eventually, I ran into kids my age and said hi. Now I call them up whenever I'm out that way. And we e-mail each other every day!

— *Roxy*

## 8. Throw a bash!

This one is my all-time favorite! I like to throw fabulous parties in my own honor. My mom lets me do it if I clean up the house and help her make all of the food. I invite lots of people in my class and in my grade. That way, I get to know lots of people all at once. And Roxy and Rella and Looie get all excited, too. We have fun meeting new folks!

— *Tutti*

# Chapter 3

# The Best Stuff About Friends!

Friends are superfab to have. They make you feel comfortable in almost any situation. They are the ones you can count on — and it feels nice to do good things for them, too. There are lots of reasons why some of your friends are everybody's favorite people. And here they are!

1. They write the notes you're excited to get.

2. They are fun to spend the night with.

3. Who else would you want to tell your juicy secrets to?

4. You hope the phone will ring — because it might be your bud.

5. Long walks and talks are better with a bud.

6. When you have a problem, you can count on them to listen.

7. They don't laugh at you when you cry at the movies.

8. E-mail from them is always awesome and comes often!

9. You can share funny inside jokes that no one else in the universe will understand.

10. You're just as at home at their houses as you are at your own.

11. It feels good to be there for them when they need you.

12. When it comes to opinions, you pretty much agree.

13. Or if you see things differently, it doesn't matter — they still love you anyway.

14. They make lunchtime at school really fun.

15. They never forget your birthday.

16. When a friend gives you a gift, you know you'll like it.

17. They'd never tell your deepest secret.

18. They always let you raid their wardrobes.

19. When you're stuck, they help you with your homework.

20. They call you from school when you're at home with the flu.

21. They help you heal a broken heart.

22. They invite you to their birthday parties.

23. You know that even if you argue, they still love you.

24. You get to have makeover slumber parties with them.

25. They understand exactly what you're going through.

Do you think your friends feel this way about you? Check out Chapter 4 to find out how to be a better buddy!

One time, some kids at school were making wisecracks about me in the lunchroom. It was Pioneer Day for my class – so I put all of this effort into my costume. I made an orange Little House on the Prairie dress all by myself. I was more dressed up than anyone else. My teacher loved my outfit, but everyone was looking at me funny all day long. Especially bullies in the lunchroom. Looie told them to stop or else. And she made me feel so much better; just that someone would do that for me was great!

# Chapter 4

# Absolutely Fabulous Ways to Be a Better Buddy

There are lots of good reasons why you need to be a great friend. One is that you want to have great friends. And they'll love you much more if you know how to treat them. We've come up with a few quick friendship tips. Keep them in mind at all times!

1. Always listen to what your friends say — even if you think you've heard them say it before. Sometimes you have to talk things over a lot to sort them out.

2. Be happy for them when they're really happy. Although it's normal to be jealous when something great happens to someone, it just feels better to be happy for them..

3. Really, sometimes your friends just want you to listen, not necessarily to hear your opinion. Try not to always give loads of advice.

4. When a friend tells you a secret, keep it! If you are ready to burst, try writing it in a journal (or, if you're like Rella, you might tell it to your cat).

5. Listen as much as you talk. The more you know about a person, the better friend you can be.

6. Never say anything about a friend that you wouldn't say to her face. There is no such thing as a part-time friend.

7. Take buddy breaks — even the best of friends need time off.

8. Let her know how you feel. When you're up-set, tell her. Things get worse if you hold them in and let them simmer. Being honest isn't easy, but it is always a very good pal policy.

9. When you're in a bad mood, it's not a good idea to take it out on your buddies.

10. Do something special for your friends. Surprise someone with her favorite candy. Or tape a movie for her from television. Or download songs she'd like and send her a singing e-mail!

# Chapter 5

# Friendship Fixes

Friend fights and troubles are far from fun. Most people would rather pull out their arm hairs than get into an argument with a friend. But even Grrrls' Girls have their tiffs. Read on for awesome advice from Rella, Tutti, Roxy, and Looie. They give you advice for all kinds of situations.

## Feeling Left Out

There's definitely one bump I've hit on the way to being buddies. When I first met the other Grrrls' Girls, they were so close that it sometimes made me feel left out. Like, they would giggle at their own inside jokes and play games I didn't know how to play. One time, they ate pizza together at Tutti's house and oops! They forgot to invite me. I was sad – I felt like I was losing the only friends I had. So here's what I did:

I decided to say something to the one person I was most comfortable talking to – Rella. I said, "Rella, is there something wrong?" Of course, she didn't know what I was talking about, so I had to put it to her point-blank. I said, "I feel so left out lately." She hugged me and said, "Oh, Looie! Why didn't you tell me?" It felt really good to finally tell her how I felt. I think I even waited way too long to say something about it. Turns out they were spending a little less time with me because I was being such a grumpster. Meanwhile, I was being a grumpster because they were leaving me out! So that didn't do anybody any good!

Rella told the others, and they made an extra effort to help me feel like one of the gang. I told them all that I was sorry for being moody, and that I would work really hard to be my old self again. Sometimes I let school and family stuff get me down. And I shouldn't take it out on my friends. But they told me that they shouldn't have been leaving me out, either. They were so sweet — they wrote me notes and said I was special. It didn't take long for things to be back to normal again.

**Friendship tip: Let your friends know if you're feeling left out.**

## Drifting Apart

I drifted apart from one of my friends at drama club. Her name was Patti. For a while, we spent a lot of time together – laughing and fooling around practicing our lines. But after a month or 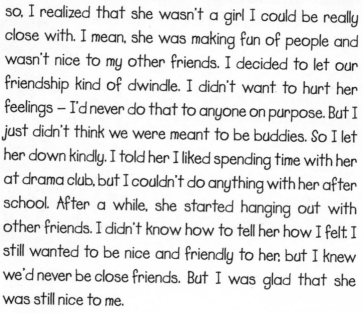 so, I realized that she wasn't a girl I could be really close with. I mean, she was making fun of people and wasn't nice to my other friends. I decided to let our friendship kind of dwindle. I didn't want to hurt her feelings – I'd never do that to anyone on purpose. But I just didn't think we were meant to be buddies. So I let her down kindly. I told her I liked spending time with her at drama club, but I couldn't do anything with her after school. After a while, she started hanging out with other friends. I didn't know how to tell her how I felt. I still wanted to be nice and friendly to her, but I knew we'd never be close friends. But I was glad that she was still nice to me.

Sometimes someone might let you drift away – and that can be sooo painful. I have had that happen to me, too. A lot of times, girls don't do it for any good reason (not like with Patti and me). Like, this one girl I knew just stopped calling me back. I knew for sure that we were no longer friends when she didn't invite me to her birthday party. I mean, what could I do? I had been really nice to her. Maybe we just didn't have enough in common. And sometimes, even if two people do like to do the same things, they might not get along the best. I was upset for a while but I got over it in time — I just decided it was her loss, not mine. And I started spending even more time with my friends who are true-blue — real Grrrls' Girls. I am lucky they are my real friends.

**Friendship tip: Don't get down when friends drift apart. Sometimes it just happens, and it's usually for the best!**

## Outsmarting Arguments

I wish life were just one big rainbow – and most of the time it is. But I'm so stubborn that I end up in arguments every once in a while. Like when Tutti is late for our shopping dates, I get really steamed. I am ticktock on time, and I don't think she even owns a watch. So one day, I bugged my mom all day long to hurry up with the errands we had to run. We had to meet Tutti at the mall at two. Well, we got there, and she didn't show up till three. I was really upset. And we didn't have any fun that day, either. She said I was too bossy. I told her she was just too selfish.

Well, we both ended up going home in a huff. And we didn't talk for another whole day. I was sad because we fought, but I was still mad at her. She felt the same way; I just know she did.

One rule we both have, though, is not to get Rella and Looie involved in our arguments. It wouldn't be fair to make them choose sides. And if I vented to them, I'd be getting them smack in the middle of it. So that's my first bit of advice – try not to talk about the person you're peeved at. I am a talker, so I have to talk it out with someone! I spill the beans to my mom – but she's the only one.

Another thing is to just give it time. After a day or so, the smoke will clear. That's when Tutti and I decided to discuss it again. Sometimes people have to wait until they can talk to each other without yelling. I mean, we know that calling each other names isn't very nice. It takes time to see things clearly. After I had cooled off, I called Tutti. I told her I needed her to try to be on time and that I didn't mean to be so bossy. She said she was sorry and she'd try.

But even if she hadn't apologized, I still would have forgiven her. I don't want to be without one of my favorite friends!

**Friendship tip: It's much easier to lose the argument than it is to lose a friend!**

# Moving Far, Far Away

I have never been through this — but I talked to some girls at school who have moved from town to town a lot. They said this is the most painful thing in the world for pals to go through. When a friend moves away, it can feel like a part of you moves with her.

From what I understand, e-mail can ease the hurt. It gives you a way to stay close to chums on the cheap. You can chat every single day without spending much money. And sometimes friends who are apart can visit each other during spring and summer vacations. The most important thing is to keep letting her know she's still special and you still care about her, even if she had to move to Singapore. Of course, she'll make new buddies eventually, but that doesn't mean you have to lose touch with each other!

There's another side to this story, too. When a new girl arrives in your class or in your neighborhood, it's important to keep in mind that she had to leave all of her best buds when she made the move with her family. It's never easy to be the new kid. It's hard to start over and not know anyone — especially when all the people who you would talk to about it (your true friends) are now far away.

A lot of times people make quick judgments about the new kid. They'll look at her clothes and other things and try to make an immediate decision whether or not she's cool. But that's not cool at all. You can't really get to know someone unless you talk to her. So, the best thing to do is be nice and ask a few questions.

Just because you are nice to someone does not mean you're committed to being her best friend. But you never know, the new girl could be someone with whom you would really get along. You should never turn down the opportunity to make a gem of a friend.

**Friendship tip: Friends are always in your heart, even if they aren't in your town.**

# Chapter 6

# You Must Have a Lot of Friends!

## Here's How to Hang With 'Em!

Sometimes you wanna hang, but you just have no clue what to do! Well, that happens to everyone. Especially when you've been friends forever, you feel like you've done everything there is to be done. But wait just one sec —that's not true.

There's always something new to go out and do! Try these tips from the Grrrls. If you're with your favorite friends, you know you'll have nothing but fun!

As you've heard before, we've got a lot of ideas — especially when it comes to palling around! Here's some stuff we think might be fun for your free afternoons:

1. If you like critters, volunteer together at an animal shelter. Or say you and your buds love shopping — have a clothing drive in your neighborhood and donate the clothes to a thrift store. You'll feel great doing stuff for other people.

   — *Rella*

2. Start an after-school dog-walking business. (Just beware of bites and loud barks! Um, maybe stick to small poochies.)

   — *Looie*

3. Write the story of how you all met, or you could write one about how you'll all still be buds in twenty years. (Each girl can write a different chapter.)

   — *Rella*

4. Have a fund-raiser. To find stuff kids can really do, go to <u>www.heavenonline.</u> It's my favorite be-sweet site. This project would take time to plan and really make work. It would be perfect for vacation.

— *Roxy*

5. Design a Web site about your favorite stars, shows, or awesome activities! If you don't know a computer whiz like Looie, buy a cheap and easy Web site-design program.

— *Tutti*

6. Make a friendship scrapbook 2gether! Or make a few — so you and your buds can each have your own.

— *Roxy*

7. Get matching temporary tattoos. Psych out your other friends and tell them the tattoos are real! (Well, it was fun, but Rella and Looie didn't believe us when Roxy and I tried this one.)

   — *Tutti*

8. Make a best-friends tune tape. Pile your CDs together and pick your favorite jammin' songs. Put them all on one tape and make copies of it for everyone!

   — *Roxy*

9. Have a picnic in a park!

   — *Looie*

10. Get together and make a fancy dinner for each of your parents. (They'll appreciate it no matter what you make.) Even make invitations for them! They'll eat it up!

   — *Rella*

11. Make a movie!!! This one is my absolute fa-
    vorite. Looie writes the script, Rella designs
    our costumes, Roxy works the camera, and I
    get to star! It's so great! If you don't have a
    video camera, you can put on a play. Our
    parents love to see what we come up with!
    — *Tutti*

12. Swing on swings — no matter how old you
    are that's a lot of fun. Push each other and
    have how-high-am-I? contests.
    — *Looie*

13. Make cool wall-sized collages. Cut up quirky
    pics from magazines and paste them on
    posterboard. Tape your collages to your
    walls — pretty soon they will be covered
    with your own art.
    — *Rella*

14. Take up a totally new hobby that *none* of you has ever done before — something like horseback riding, sailing, playing an instrument, or fishing!

— **Looie**

15. Looie made me put this one down: Next time it rains, put on old grubby clothes and go bike riding! Crash through mud puddles and splash your pals as much as possible.

— **Rella**

16. Go see your favorite movie during the theater's off-hours. If no one else is there, you can talk and laugh like you're at home!

— **Tutti**

17. Watch Little League kids play ball in the summer. It's a great way to meet their older sibs. And it can be really funny, too!

— **Roxy**

18. Set up a car-wash Saturday. Put signs up all over your neighborhood announcing your car wash and where it is. Use the money for a special friend party — or donate it to a local charity.

— *Roxy*

19. Get out your favorite little-kid toys and pictures. Swap stories about how much you loved your walking-talking puppy or about your first-ever birthday party! It's a great way to get to know your buds better!

— *Rella*

20. Go thrift shopping as a group. Try on goofy old clothes! And if you really wanna have fun, buy one of those old video games called Atari. They're so cheap and funny!

— *Roxy*

# Chapter 7

# Real Answers for Real Pal Problems

Friends should be concerned about people and their problems. It's hard to know what to do when things get kinda screwy! So the Grrrls wanted to share some answers to the most-asked questions kids have about friendships — from school stuff to sleepovers!

**Q:** My BFF and I always argue lately. How can we get along like we used to?

**A:** Hi! It's Roxy. Fighting is bad — especially when you do it with your best bud. Maybe you're at each other's throats because you're both a little moody? It seems like pals often make the mistake of taking their problems out on the ones they love — each other. Is there new and stressful stuff going on in her life, or in yours? If that's the case, you just need to have a heart-to-heart. Tell her you're sorry for snapping — it's just because you've got a lot on your mind. Chances are, she'll say the exact same thing to you. Sometimes you just get too used to your best friend, and you take each other for granted. So it's good to give each other a little bit of space. Spend some peaceful time alone. You may need it to think through your stress. And you know, it's true that absence makes the heart grow fonder, especially when it comes to friendships! You'll miss her so much that you'll be back to normal in no time!

**Q:** I think my friend and I like the same boy, but I really want him to like me. I don't want to lose her as a friend!

**A:** Boy, oh, boy — you've got a problem! This is Rella, by the way. Guys do get in the way of friendships sometimes, even when they shouldn't. I would say you have to be up front with your friend and tell her what's going on. If you keep this a secret, it will come between you in the long run. So talk it out!

Make sure you're honest with her because the bottom line is, boyfriends may not last, but friends are forever!

**Q:** My friend copies my every move. I don't know what to do!

**A:** First of all, even though you're frustrated, take time to be flattered! I know a lot about style — this is Tutti, by the way — and this means you've got it! That's why she copies you and your style.

This is tricky territory. If you say something to her, she could take it the wrong way. You don't want to trash her feelings. So here's what I'd do: I'd try shopping with her one day. Then when she picks out the same stuff as you, you can speak up. Say something like, "We really need to make an effort to stop wearing so much stuff alike. People at school are saying things behind our backs! I don't want them to make fun of us!" Now, I realize that you may not care what people at school say — but putting it to your copycat pal this way may spare her feelings. And you'll still get the message across that you want to remain unique! You could even pick out some clothes that would look amazing on her. She might just need some advice.

**Q:** I clam up around kids my age. How can I be *not* shy?

**A:** Hi, I'm Looie, and I know what you're going through. I can be shy, too. I try to be more out-going by practicing talking to people I don't know. Choose a girl who smiles a lot and looks happy. You know, someone sweet like Rella! Tell your nerves to hush the heck up. Just walk up to her and say, "Hi!" Plan something to talk about, too, so you won't be tongue-tied. You know, ask her if she has a cat, or if she saw that great new movie. Chances are, she'll warm up to you! And the more times you practice this, the better you'll get at it —and the less shy you'll feel! Believe me, I'm still working on it! But I'm getting better and becoming a chatter. Well, almost!

**Q:** I have a friend who's too bossy. It seems like we always do what she wants to do. Help!

**A:** This is Tutti. Ooooh, girl! You've got to put your pal in her place — politely, though! I know because I've been guilty of being too bossy. Your friend probably doesn't realize that she's bumming you out. She probably thinks she's doing you a favor by coming up with things to do and keeping you busy. I know I didn't have a clue when I was telling everyone what to do. I used to plan Roxy and Rella and Looie's whole weekend. We'd go shopping, then act out plays, and then we'd watch my favorite flicks at my place. I was in heaven, but they were, well, bored. Roxy finally pulled me aside and said, "I really wanna do some different stuff, like Rollerblade and ride bikes. Let's try that for a change. After all, it's our turn to choose what we do!" I got the hint! But I'm glad she spoke up, or else I would have gotten out of control!

So you have to set your pal straight. Just make sure you offer options of other things to do. For example, if she always chooses who you hang out with, tell her which girls *you* want to see. Get it? She'll figure out exactly what you have in mind. Now, I'm not saying she'll never get out of hand again — I know sometimes I do —but at least she'll make an effort to tone herself down.

**Q:** I feel like my two friends are edging me out. What can I do?

**A:** You must be sad in this situation. This is Looie, and I am sorry a sweet girl like you has to go through it. Feel free to hang out with me! But first, make sure you're right about your pals. Are they purposely not inviting you places? Are they doing things together, then lying about it to you later? Have they stopped calling you back? If any of these things have happened more than once, then you just might be right. It's not fun, either! So I'd say to start hanging out with truer-bluer buds! If you need to make new friends, just check out our tips in Chapter 5. But still be nice to your old crew. Maybe they'll come around and see what they're missin' — you! In the meantime, pal around with other people. Spend your time with someone who wants to spend her time with you. Before you know it, you'll have much more important things to do than worry about old friends.

**Q:** My friend is too worried about her weight, and we're only twelve! Should I tell her mom?
**A:** My big sis went through this. I just don't understand why girls don't see their beauty! They should ask me, Roxy — I'd tell 'em. Anyway, It's way too bad that girls worry about their bodies so often. Your friend is not alone. Maybe it's best to let *your* mom know what's going on.

All you can do is just be a good friend. Your buddy needs to know that you love her — AS IS! And that you'll be there to help her through it no matter what!

**Q:** My friend spilled my crush secret. Now everyone knows who I like, and I am steamin' mad. What should I do?

**A:** This is Rella. I'll answer this one — it's a toughie. I would definitely sit your friend down and have a nice long talk. I mean, she's really putting your friendship at stake if she's violating your trust. Basically, she needs to realize what she did. But don't tell her that she's a bad, awful bud. Instead, just tell her how you feel. Say something like, "I am so hurt about my secret getting out. I am embarrassed, and I don't feel like I can trust you." Hopefully, she'll apologize. And in the future, you'll know this girl isn't very good at keeping a secret. Sometimes even really great friends let things slip — people make mistakes. So give her time to earn your trust back; if she's a really great friend, she deserves another chance! 👑

## See Ya! Bye!

Rella and Roxy and Tutti and Looie want to thank you for being a good friend. They hope you learned a thing or two that will help you to be a better bud! That would make them smile really wide!

Look for other 2 Grrrls tips in upcoming books. Don't forget to check out their Web site at www.2grrrls.com!